3/99

D1507970

14.95

At the Grocery Store

Illustrations

Penny Dann

Picture Credits

© Andy Sacks/Tony Stone Images: 30
© Bette. S. Garber/Highway Images: 26
© Don & Pat Valenti/Tony Stone Images: 4, 20
© 1994 Gary Bublitz/Dembinsky Photo Assoc. Inc: 6
© Jack McConnell: 8, 16, 18, 22
© Jeff Zaruba/Tony Stone Images: cover, 14
© Jon Gray/Tony Stone Images: 3
© Rex. A. Butcher/Tony Stone Images: 24
© Robert E. Daemmrich/Tony Stone Worldwide: 10, 12
© Tom Tracy/Tony Stone Images: 28

Library of Congress Cataloging-in-Publication Data

Greene, Carol.

At the grocery store / by Carol Greene.
p. cm.
Summary: Describes, in simple text, what a grocery
store is, the kinds of items that it sells,
and the people who work there.
ISBN 1-56766-565-9 (lib. bdg. : alk. paper)
1. Grocery trade—Juvenile literature.
[1. Grocery trade.] I. Title.

HD9320.5.G728   1998   98-13476
381'.148—dc21   CIP
                            AC

At the Grocery Store

By Carol Greene

The Child's World®, Inc.

Grocery stores make shopping easy for people. They offer lots of foods to choose from. Some stores stay open all the time, too.

Grocery stores sell lots of food for lots of people.

HMMMM!

People who work in grocery stores like to help others. What if you can't find something? The workers can help you.

Grocery store workers know where everything is.

CRINKLE! RUSTLE!

Grocery store workers keep the store clean, too. They straighten the groceries. They make sure all the food is fresh.

MMMM!

Some stores have a **bakery**. Good smells come from here. Workers bake fresh bread and goodies all day.

Bakers make everything from fresh bread to fancy cakes.

Fruits and vegetables are called **produce**. They are kept in special cases.

HSSSS!

Water sprays from the top of the cases. This keeps the produce fresh and crispy.

This person works in the **deli**. Delis sell sausage, cheese, salads, and other special foods. They can make you a great sandwich.

"Deli" is short for "delicatessen."

This is the meat counter. It holds things such as beef, chicken, pork, and fish. The cases are cold to keep the meat fresh.

Meat counters hold hamburger, sausage, and bologna.

Dairy products need special cases, too. The milk and cheese must stay cool and dry. Dairy companies bring fresh products often.

Dairy products do not last long. If they do not sell quickly, they must be thrown out.

Much of the food in a grocery store sits on shelves. The shelves hold cereal, soup, cookies, and other foods. Workers check the shelves often to make sure they are neat and full.

The shelves also list the prices of the foods.

Sometimes stores have special sales. They also set up nice-looking **displays**. Why? To bring more people into the store.

Big stores sell more than just food. They also sell toys, books, cards, crayons, hats, and much more.

VROOM! PSSHH! BEEP!

**Trucks pull up to the dock.
They bring the groceries the
store needs.**

Sometimes the groceries
come in heavy boxes.
Machines called forklifts
lift the boxes off the truck.

WHIRR! TAP! RUSTLE!

The checkout counter is where people pay for the things they are buying.

Sometimes people put their own groceries into bags. In other stores, workers do that for them.

Here is the store manager. He is in charge of the whole store! He makes sure everything is fresh and clean. He makes sure the customers are happy, too.

The store manager has a very busy job.

GLOSSARY

bakery (BAY–ker–ee)
A bakery makes breads, rolls, and cakes. Some grocery stores have bakeries inside.

deli (DEH–lee)
A deli sells meats, cheeses, and other special foods.

displays (dih–SPLAYZ)
A display is a nice way of arranging things. Some stores make displays to sell special things.

dock (DOK)
The dock is where trucks drop things off. Trucks that come to the docks carry different foods.

produce (PROH–doos)
Produce is another name for fruits and vegetables. Produce must be kept cool.

INDEX

CAROLE GREENE has published over 200 books for children. She also likes to read books, make teddy bears, work in her garden, and sing. Ms. Greene lives in Webster Groves, Missouri.